Nancy & Howard —

The experience of living in your special
house has been so magical for me. The
lake, the volcanoes, sun, stars, moon, fishermen
telling stories in the middle of the night while
fishing. Thank you so for sharing it with me.

Warmest regards,

Nanci

t 2, 1977

Aguacatán

THE *Highland Maya*

Patterns of Life and Clothing in Indian Guatemala

Text by Roland Bunch

Photographs by Roger Bunch

Cover photo: San Juan Sacatepéquez. Market scene

Back cover: Lake Atitlán

Dedicated to the indigenous peoples of the Americas

in hopes that they will

be able to shape for themselves

the brighter future they deserve.

Nebaj. Easter procession

Contents

Preface

Every culture must develop its own ways of eating and dressing, of earning a living, of dealing with friends and relatives, and of courting, marrying, and raising children. Each society must decide on its own ways of expressing feelings, of explaining the known and the unknown, of exercising authority and enforcing it, and, finally, of passing all these patterns on to new generations. It takes hundreds of years of trial and error to create a culture. For ancient peoples never had scientific laboratories where, in a few weeks or months, new customs could be tested under carefully controlled conditions and then disseminated to millions of people in the form of a book or television documentary. The laboratory that traditional cultures used was the world; their experimental design was life itself; and their standard of success was, in some cases, the culture's very survival.

I have long been captivated by the enormous, age-old structures mankind has built through the centuries to honor his God or gods. I find that I feel the same fascination whether I am standing before a medieval Gothic cathedral in France, a multi-minareted mosque in Calcutta, or an eighteenth century wat in Bangkok. Each one of these buildings is a lasting monument to the care and dedication of a people, to decades of skilled craftsmanship and hard, back-breaking work. They each have a unique, ornate complexity, yet this complexity is symmetrical and balanced. The diversity is held together by a subtle unity.

Ancient cultures, like ancient cathedrals, show the results of decades of effort, care, and artistry. Cultures, too, have an unexpected complexity. (I can remember I used to think that only my own North American culture had finally ridded itself of "customs" and adopted a simple, straightforward way of life. But then one day in a little corner bookstore in Kyoto, I ran across a book that spent over 500 pages explaining to the Japanese people the bewildering customs of the North American.) Still, there is unity in all this diversity. Cultures, too, must have a symmetry, a consistency in their values and actions. The quiet, deeply religious dances of Thailand have much in common with the gentle people who created them, just as Tahitian dances pulsate with the carefree, sensuous nature of the people of the South Pacific, and Japanese dances show the highly developed esthetic sense and controlled emotions of the Japanese. Hindu music could no more be confused with Haitian music than the Guatemalan *trajes* pictured in this book could be mistaken for a sari, a kimono, or a Roy Halston tennis dress.

Yet the world's ancient temples, for all their awe-inspiring artistry, have a weathered, dingy look, as if they were partially abandoned. The massive columns and meter-thick walls give them a heavy, cumbersome feel no longer necessary with today's technology of steel and glass. Efficiency of space, lighting, and upkeep was never among their virtues.

Old, traditional cultures often have a weathered, dingy look about them, too. Their slow, cumbersome heaviness makes them inefficient, leaving them ill-suited to compete with today's moneyed multinationals and computer-planned factories. And the resulting poverty adds to their over-all impression of weight and darkness.

Once I enter a cathedral's huge, weathered doors, however, the atmosphere changes. I suddenly feel an unmistakable desire to be quiet, to tiptoe, to take off my shoes and walk in stockinged feet. Partly to avoid disturbing those around me, and partly out of reverence, I begin to wish I could remain unseen and unheard. Even if I have all afternoon to gaze with wide-eyed curiosity, I start feeling cheated because there won't be enough time to see all there is to see and learn all there is to learn.

The feeling is much the same when I begin getting to know a new culture. For all the dirt and grime that looked so uninviting from the outside, the inside always seems worthy of reverence and respect. In spite of the heaviness and inefficiency so apparent from the outside, I find that, once inside, I want to become invisible, to leave behind my towering North American frame and

San Juan Comalapa

watch and learn from those around me. For the economic position of a culture does not affect my respect for it any more than the lack of central heating and a marble-white exterior distracts from my feeling for a Gothic cathedral. Why should a culture's per capita gross national product have anything to do with its value as a work of art—or source of wisdom?

Years of living and working among traditional cultures have convinced me that every group of people has a good deal to teach every other group—a lot that could help other groups, including our own, to live more happily. A friend once told me that the best indication that we have stopped discriminating against another group is that we begin wanting to learn from them. I would add that the moment at which we begin to learn from them is the moment at which we begin to live richer, fuller, more satisfying lives.

So Roger and I decided to produce this book. In part we have done it as a challenge and as an adventure. But more than that, we have done it because we hope that some of those from outside Guatemala will learn a little more about a culture that has taught us a great deal—and will come to appreciate and respect a culture we have grown to love.

THE PICTURES

One of the first things visitors to Guatemala notice about the Indian people is their dress, or *traje*. The variety and colorfulness of these *trajes* is almost without rival elsewhere in the world; more than 100 different traditional outfits are worn in an area the size of New Hampshire. Still largely woven on traditional back-strap looms, these clothes vary in shape, color, design, type of weave, and method of use, all depending on the home towns of their wearers.

In selecting the *trajes* to be illustrated in this book, we have included outfits with a variety of colors, weaves, and designs, as well as a wide geographic spread. The *trajes* pictured here are not necessarily the oldest, most traditional styles known today, nor even the oldest ones in present use. They are, instead, styles commonly worn as everyday dress—styles that any visitor to Guatemala could expect to see if he visited the towns from which they come. Some of the outfits, like those from Chichicastenango and San Juan Sacatepéquez, will be recognized by the most casual visitor to Guatemala, while others may be a surprise even to the amateur collector of Indian *trajes*.

We have given priority to showing a way of life, rather than to illustrating all the intricacies of Indian clothes, because we feel that the *trajes* can best be appreciated when seen as an integral part of a way of life—just as a medieval statue commands more respect in its fourteenth century cathedral than it does when moved to a twentieth century museum.

A good many friends have contributed to the making of this book. Stanley Kramer and Lynn Richardson Turner first taught us of the beauties of other peoples. During the months after the earthquake in Guatemala when very few homes in the Chimaltenango area were habitable, the Marcelo Zúniga and Tomás Fuentes families fed and housed us. We would like to thank William Decker for providing invaluable suggestions on the writing, and John Alexander for his help during the printing of the pictures. And, of course, our parents, Dodds and Mildred Bunch, have given us help and encouragement throughout the process of making the book.

But most of all, we want to thank the dozens of Guatemalan Indian people who appear in the pictures of this book. The beauty we have tried to capture in these pages is, in truth, their beauty.

Roland Bunch
January, 1977

Introduction

HISTORY OF THE HIGHLAND MAYA

The origin of the Mayan people remains a mystery. We do not know where they came from or even who they were. Yet before Rome was founded, they had established a sophisticated, cosmopolitan culture in the highlands of present-day Guatemala. By the first century A. D., the inhabitants of Kaminaljuyú, near Guatemala City, had developed notable skills in painting, ceramics, architecture, and astronomy, and were using the only system of writing that originated in the Western Hemisphere.

One would expect that with such a promising start and a favorable environment, the civilization of the highland Maya would have developed into one of the major civilizations of Middle America. Yet after 150 A. D., the highland Maya never again used their system of hieroglyphic writing, nor did they ever build another city of the architectural grandeur of Kaminaljuyú.

What had happened? Why did the highland Maya go into decline at just the time that another Mayan group a few hundred miles to the north was building the foundations of a Golden Age which would rival that of the greatest civilizations of its time? Furthermore, why did one Mayan group, which enjoyed the advantages of fertile soils, an invigorating climate, and a wealth of natural resources, fail to progress, while their cousins in the hot, disease- and insect-ridden rain forests of the Petén became the Western Hemisphere's leading scholars?

The most recent archeological findings lead us to believe that the highland Maya failed to accomplish more precisely because theirs *was* such an inviting area. From the time of Christ on, one group after another set out southward from Mexico looking for land to settle. Repeated waves of immigrants passed through the highlands, subduing the peoples they found in their way and either settling down or continuing southeastward into Salvador, Honduras, and Nicaragua. With each invasion, the scholars, priests, and rulers of the area were annihilated, their learning, religions, and governments supplanted by those of their conquerors. But whereas the aristocracy of the cities were the vanquished, the peasant people, spread out among their cornfields, served as the spoils. Passive and unorganized, the rural farmers were left to provide food and cheap labor for a new set of masters. Thus with each successive invasion, the sophisticated learning, the specialized art forms, and the advanced religious concepts of each group were lost, while the ethnic and linguistic heritage of the Mayan masses survived for over two thousand years.

The scant evidence we have indicates that the first of the invading groups came from Teotihuacán, the well-known city of the Pyramid to the Sun near Mexico City. These invaders probably began moving through the highlands around 400 A. D., for within 200 years of that date, they had largely rebuilt the city of Kaminaljuyú, a la Teotihuacán. And they may well have been responsible for the loss of the Mayan hieroglyphs from the highland area.

About five hundred years later, another group from Mexico began moving through the highlands. This time they came from the famed Mexican city of Tulán, domain of the great god-king Quetzalcoatl. With them they brought their Toltec gods, their legends and historical traditions, and their religious practices, including human sacrifice. Once again the invaders replaced the learned classes of the cities but left the peasant farmers to till their fields. In time, the oral history and legends of the Mexican conquerors became part of the intellectual traditions of a culture, the majority of which was Mayan in language and ethnic background. The highland Maya, whose roots in Guatemala extend back over two thousand years, came to accept as their own the history recorded in the *Popol Vuh* and *Annals of the Cakchiquels*, which tell of migrating from central Mexico well after 700 A. D.

Another five hundred years passed, and another group of invaders swept through the highlands. Once again, the invaders came southward from central Mexico. Again they destroyed the

Sacapulas. Putting on a hairpiece ᵣ

cities, dispersed or killed the ruling classes, and established their own religious traditions. With this invasion, the same hieroglyphs that had previously disappeared from the highlands perished from the lowlands to the north as well. Yet once again the Mayan peasantry quietly persisted. Valued as ever for their cheap labor and agricultural produce, the Mayan people managed to preserve their language, their ethnic identity, and even traces of their ancient religions. This time, the Mayan culture had withstood the onslaught of two of the mightiest powers on the face of the earth—the Spanish Empire and the Roman Catholic Church.

THE HIGHLAND MAYA TODAY

Most of the 2½ million Mayan people still live scattered across the highlands area that extends from Guatemala City north and west to the Mexican border. Nearly all of them speak one or more of the twenty Mayan languages still in use, and virtually all of them still grow corn and beans, squash, or one of the other traditional Mayan foods. The region they live in varies from 4,000 to over 10,000 feet in elevation and enjoys a cool, temperate climate. Its rolling hills and undulating plateaus are frequently cut by deep, vertically-walled river valleys. Along the southern border of the highlands runs a chain of more than a dozen volcanoes, some of which periodically become active, sending rivers of red and yellow lava down their slopes and spreading new fertile layers of volcanic dust across the highlands.

THE INDIAN *TRAJE*

Many people in Guatemala claim that the *trajes* (pronounced TRAH Heys) worn by the Indian people today were created by the Spanish and imposed upon the Indian people in order to control their movement from one town to another. But most of the *trajes* worn by the Indian people today resemble those worn by the Mayan elite of pre-conquest Tikal and Yaxchilán much more than they do anything ever worn by the Spanish. Furthermore, some sixteenth century Spanish authors, like Francisco Antonio de Fuentes y Guzmán, denied that the Spanish had had to modify very many of the highlands outfits. Although the Spanish colonial government may have dictated some variations from town to town, the Indian people have since then undoubtedly modified their clothes beyond recognition. In some towns, the *huipiles,* or hand-woven blouses, worn today show almost no similarity to those of just fifty years ago.

In any case, the *trajes* of today are a wonder of pragmatic simplicity. The *huipil* (pronounced Wee PEEL) consists of nothing more than two or three rectangular pieces of cloth that are joined together with holes either cut or left unsewn for the head and arms. *Huipiles* are generally made larger than the wearer and then adjusted to fit more snugly by gathering or pleating them down both sides. Since sizes are flexible and styles change slowly, a woman can wear the same garment from the time she is fifteen years old to over fifty. Nor does pregnancy or nursing cause any problems. Depending upon the custom of the town in which she lives, a woman may nurse her baby by opening a slit in the center of the *huipil,* by letting the baby nurse through the arm hole, or by pulling the whole baby up under her *huipil.*

The men's *trajes,* except in the areas of Lake Atitlán and Huehuetenango, have largely disappeared. In many cases a hand-woven red sash worn as a belt is the only piece of clothing left to identify a man as an Indian.

Trajes vary markedly from one *municipio,* or township, to another, so that a person who knows the different styles can easily tell from what town an Indian woman comes. Most often, the colors or designs of the *huipil* indicate the traje's origin. Other times the *traje* can be identified by the width of the *huipil's* stripes, the color, length, or fullness of the skirt, or the colors or designs in the belt or carrying cloth. By using the photographs and the appendix in this book, even those people unfamiliar with Indian clothes should be able to identify the origin of most of the *trajes* worn in Guatemala.

THE TASK-SIMPLE CULTURE

Those people fortunate enough to stay in Guatemala longer than a few weeks frequently begin noticing certain characteristics of the Indian people themselves. Many people comment about the Indians' quiet sense of dignity and pride. Others notice the people's passivity, the rareness with which they become angry, and the eager obedience of their children. When I first visited Guatemala, I was also struck by these qualities of the Indian people. But I have been even more surprised by the recurrence of these same characteristics among the world's peasant peoples almost anywhere I have gone, from Ponape to Kathmandu

Left: *Santa María Chiquimula*

Right: *Zunil*

Below: *Santiago Chimaltenango,*
Huehuetenango

and from Cape Haitian to Mandalay. These characteristics are found to some degree in almost all traditional cultures; the "culture of poverty" is world-wide.

Gradually I have come to suspect that one of the most important features of most traditionally oriented, slowly changing cultures is that *the skills that one must master in order to function well within the society are relatively few in number and easy to learn.* Many very important cultural traits seem to trace their origins to this one central fact, which I shall call "task simplicity."

First of all, a member of a task-simple culture seldom has to face the prospect of failure; he can generally enjoy a feeling of supreme competence. Almost any woman can learn to make corn tortillas, fry beans, wash and mend clothes, and take care of her children. She learns these skills early in life because she helps her mother with them from the time she is able to walk and because there are only a few such skills for her to learn. She need not worry about how to cook vegetables, make fancy salads, iron or bleach her clothes, or raise her children according to Dr. Spock. Furthermore, her mother fries beans in the same way she will be expected to prepare them in the future. There is no chance that her neighbors will have different, better ways of frying beans, or that some magazine will come out with a new, improved recipe. She can easily be completely and irrevocably competent at the skills her society expects her to master by the time she begins wanting to set up her own household.

When she does marry, her new husband has every reason to feel equally competent at a man's skills—planting corn and beans, cutting firewood, and tending the animals. Until such new-fangled ideas as fertilizers, crop rotations, and animal vaccines come along and change things, he, too, can feel perfectly capable of handling the tasks expected of him. How would it feel in our society if one were completely sure that he could pass every examination with a perfect score, succeed at any occupation he might choose, and have no difficulty fixing the car, tending the garden, feeding the children, or handling any other job that might confront him? Is it at all surprising that Indian people seem to have a sense of self-confidence and dignity?

A second result of the task simplicity of a culture is that competition is reduced to a minimum. If everyone could spell perfectly, there would be no use in holding spelling bees. Likewise, if everyone in a culture has performed the same easily learned skills in the same way for many years, little room is left for competition. Of course, certain kinds of competition, especially in social relations and the marketplace, will still exist. But in Indian society, as in many traditional societies, even social competition is held to a minimum by the firmly established social categories within the community and the lack of social contact with those outside the community.

Task simplicity also serves to minimize criticism within a society. If everyone grows corn equally well, in the same, age-old manner, no one will have the opportunity or desire to find fault with his neighbor's cornfield. As a result, Indian people can, to an amazing degree, live without criticism. In fact, many outsiders who work with them notice before long their extreme sensitivity to any kind of disapproval, their reluctance to find fault with anyone else (except with those they do not like, and then only in their absence), and their elaborate means of communicating disapproval to each other when they must (usually through a series of intermediaries). Obviously, they are not accustomed to dealing with criticism.

Lastly, task simplicity can also contribute to the quiet passivity often observed in Indian people. Frustration is the result of a person's not being able to reach some goal toward which he is striving. In a traditional, task-simple society, one seldom aspires to a goal not already accepted by the society—for fear of social disapproval and for want of examples among those one looks up to. Those goals that *are* acceptable within the culture usually have easily mastered, well-defined methods of attainment. People in task-simple societies, therefore, rarely experience frustration. Inasmuch as frustration is the normal cause of anger and anger the most frequent cause of violence, people who experience only small quantities of frustration seldom erupt into anger and violence.

Thus task simplicity in a culture can lead to a sense of self-confidence and a minimum of competition, criticism, frustration, anger, and violence. Of course, no culture can exist without some anger, competition, and feelings of inadequacy. Competition will exist to some degree in every culture, and, for the extremely poor, not being able to buy the food necessary for good health can be immensely frustrating. Furthermore, the Indian people, like most other traditional people, have begun changing and acquiring new skills.

But the complexity of even the slowly changing task-simple

cultures is nothing when compared to that of the world's industrial societies. In these cultures, it seems, new and more complicated skills are needed every day; few people ever become truly competent at any one vocation and then only after years of education and single-minded dedication; and values and tastes are so numerous and transitory that even those people who spend a lifetime mastering a skill may find it is no longer appreciated. When we compare these societies to traditional cultures, even traditional cultures now beginning to change, the differences are still immense.

San Martin Jilotepeque

HIGHLANDS GUATEMALA

Trajes of numbered towns appear in the book

1. San Ildefonso Ixtahuacán (p. 81)
2. Santiago Chimaltenango (p. 6)
3. San Juan Atitán (pp. 66-7)
4. Todos Santos Cuchumatán (pp. 64-5)
5. San Mateo Ixtatán (p. 77)
6. Soloma (p. 54)
7. Aguacatán (Frontispiece)
8. Nebaj (p. vi)
9. Chajul (pp. 14-5)
10. San Juan Cotzal (p. 34)
11. Sacapulas (p. 3)
12. Cobán (p. 78)
13. Rabinal (pp. 24-5)
14. San Juan Sacatepéquez (Cover)
15. Santo Domingo Xenacoj (pp. 36-7)
16. Santa María de Jesús (p. 21)
17. San Antonio Aguas Calientes (p. 55)
18. San Martín Jilotepeque (p. 11)
19. Joyabaj (p. 70)
20. Zacualpa (p. 22)
21. San Juan Comalapa (p. x)
22. San Antonio Nejapa (p. 49)
23. Tecpán (p. 69)
24. Patzum (p. 41)
25. Santo Tomás Chichicastenango (p. 63)
26. San Antonio Palopó (p. 57)
27. Santa Catarina Palopó (pp. 33)
28. Sololá (pp. 26-7)
29. Santiago Atitlán (pp. 38-9)
30. San Pedro La Laguna (p. 52)
31. Nahualá (pp. 58,84)
32. Santa María Chiquimula (p. 6)
33. Zunil (p. 7)
34. Almolonga (p. 50)
35. Quezaltenango (Xelajú) (p. 72)
36. San Martín Sacatepéquez
    (Chile Verde) (p. 42)
37. San Pedro Sacatepéquez (p. 47)

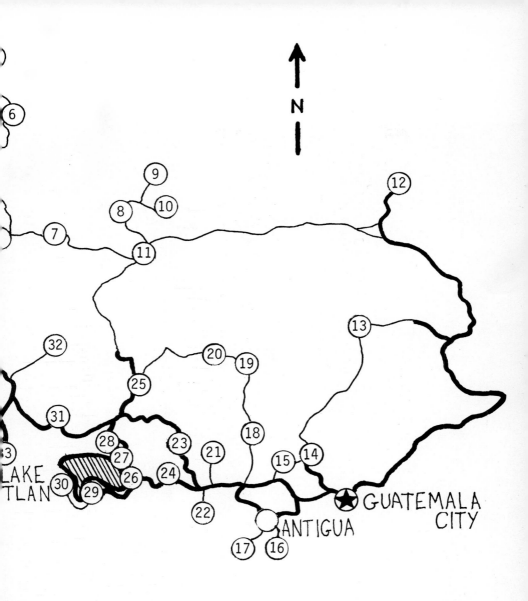

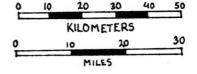

Shaded area of map at
left is enlarged above

1
CORN, SOIL, AND SWEAT

Chajul. Making tortillas

The ancient Maya estimated the trajectory of planets with an error of less than one minute in four years. They regularly predicted eclipses of the sun and moon, developed a calendar as accurate as the one we use today, and independently discovered the zero—a feat matched by only two other civilizations in history. The precursors of the Aztecs built pyramids as large as those in Egypt, and the Incas organized systems of agricultural development and social welfare that rival any seen in the Western world before this century.

Nevertheless, within a hundred years after the Spanish Conquest, the pyramids had been abandoned, the mathematics and astronomy forgotten, and the social organization destroyed. Of the splendor once achieved by America's pre-Columbian peoples, all that seemed to remain were jungle-enshrouded monuments, crumbling irrigation ditches, and a quiet, enigmatic peasant people.

Yet perhaps the greatest achievement of Indian society—in fact, the very one that made all the others possible—is the one that has also proven the most durable: the simple corn plant. We do not know when, where, or even how the Indian people acquired it. But somehow, by the time Columbus sailed his ships, they had populated two continents with one of the most remarkable plants mankind has ever used to feed himself.

The mysterious origins of the corn plant could be most easily established, of course, if some wild varieties of corn could be found. Yet scientists have spent careers searching for such a plant—to no avail. Corn remains the world's only major grain that has no known wild prototypes.

The few faint clues to corn's origins that we do have are faint indeed. They include such archeological finds as three 5,600-year-old, thimble-sized corn cobs found in a cave in central Mexico and a few dozen pollen grains brought up in a drill core from 200 feet below the Palace of Fine Arts in the center of Mexico City. Upon these and other equally shaky foundations, scientists have constructed their theories. But, in fact, corn's origins are still wrapped in mystery. If its ancestors were originally developed from some kind of wild corn that has since died out, someone must explain why it disappeared. If it was developed by crossing or improving some not-too-distant relatives, evidence of the relatives and their descendency or susceptibility to crossing should be found.

By whatever means the Indian people acquired the corn plant, they rapidly began adapting it to their needs. They gradually increased the size of the ear (from about the size of a good head of wheat) and developed a husk that protected the ear from insects and birds. In the process, they may have ended the plant's ability to survive in a wild state. With no one to tear open the husk and spread the seeds, the ubiquitous corn plant would more than likely have disappeared from the face of the earth within two or three years.

During this more than 5,000-year process of upbreeding the corn plant, the Indian people also developed an impressive array of different varieties. Corn plants range in height from two feet to over twenty. They can mature any time from 60 days to over 11 months after planting, and can, from a single seed, produce as many as 15 stalks. The corn plant is so versatile that it can be grown commercially all the way from the windswept prairies of Canada to the tropical rain forests of Zaire, and from the cold northern steppes of Russia to the humid jungles of Panama. It thrives anywhere from below sea level near the Caspian Sea to over 13,000 feet in elevation on the Peruvian *altiplano,* and with anything from 10 to over 400 inches of rainfall a year. Corn holds the distinction of being the most widely adapted cereal crop known to man.

But the real value of any food plant lies in its ability to produce food. Here, again, corn has few peers. As early as the Spanish Conquest, corn was already the most prolific grain crop ever cultivated by man. Early sixteenth century European herbalists, describing a grain few of their readers had ever seen, wrote about varieties of corn nearly as productive as those we use today:

> Only one stalk grows from each grain. Often, however, one stalk bears two and three ears, and one ear bears 100 and 200, 400 and even as many as 600 grains.

What other cereal plant can regularly produce from 1,000 to as many as 2,000 grains for each seed planted? Corn was then, and continues to be, more efficient at converting the sun's energy into human food than any other crop on earth. Five hundred years before twentieth century scientists received the Nobel Peace Prize for spurring a "green revolution" with varieties of "miracle wheat" and "miracle rice," the Indian people of the Americas had already developed the world's first miracle grain—corn.

But the corn plant was to exert every bit as much impact upon the history of the Indian people as the Indian people did upon the history of corn. For a civilization can grow and blossom only when its farmers can grow more food than their own families need. If a farmer's family eats everything he can produce, no food will be left over for pyramid-builders and priests, scholars and teachers, soldiers and statesmen. The first item of business for any civilization must be that of producing a surplus of food.

To produce such a surplus, most emerging civilizations received a generous assist from Mother Nature. In one location after another, huge, gently moving rivers flowed through flat-bottomed valleys with pleasant, invigorating climates. The rich alluvial soils and temperate climates provided ideal conditions for almost any grain, and the rivers obligingly overflowed at the end of each growing season to provide new soils and nutrients for the following year. Under such conditions, producing surpluses was a relatively simple matter, so that before long, those surpluses were feeding scholars and teachers, soldiers and statesmen. Civilizations sprang up along the Hwang Ho and the Nile, the Tigris and the Euphrates, the Chao Phrya and the Brahmaputra.

In Middle and South America, few such ideal environments were to be found. The major rivers were tropical, disease-ridden, and swampy. Anyone who tried to cultivate their rich bottom-lands would likely as not have his crops washed away by unpredictable floodwaters. Any would-be founders of civilizations in the Americas would have to come up with a different means of producing surpluses—a highly productive food plant and a technology to make it grow well, year after year.

The plant, of course, was corn. The technology varied according to the climate and terrain. On the parched Peruvian coast, hundreds of miles of irrigation ditches far superior to those in use there today carried water to the dry, sandy fields. In the steep-sloped Andes, extensive systems of terraces protected the hillsides from erosion. Soil fertility was maintained through the use of 10- to 15-year periods of fallow (similar to those used today by the Mayan Indians on the Yucatán Peninsula), through burying fish next to the seeds, or by intercropping corn with nitrogen-fixing field beans.

A wide assortment of varieties also had to be developed. For the Maya would need disease-resistant, hot-weather varieties that could withstand heavy rainfalls before they would be able to build their civilization in the lowland jungles of the Petén. Temperate-climate plants with limited water requirements would be needed so the Toltec and Aztec Empires could thrive in central Mexico. And cold-weather, high-altitude varieties would have to be developed to provide their share (along with "Irish" potatoes and quinoa) of the economic base of the fabulous 2½-mile-high Inca Empire.

The varieties were developed and the civilizations prospered. And the people reverently recognized the corn plant's importance. Legends preserved in the *Popol Vuh* of the Quiché-Maya nation tell a creation story in which the gods formed man out of corn dough rather than clay. Another legend tells of Quetzalcoatl, the great feathered-serpent god of the Toltecs, bringing civilization to the Americas in the guise of corn. Fifteenth century Europeans recognized the importance of the Indian people's achievement, too. Within one generation of Columbus' first voyage, corn had spread throughout southern Europe; within two generations, it had spread around the world.

Today corn, along with rice and wheat, shares the honor of being among the world's three most important crops. Worldwide, nearly a quarter of a billion acres of it are planted each year. It is grown in well over half the nations of the world, and on every continent except Antarctica. Corn continues to be a staple food for major populations in Africa and Latin America, while in the United States it occupies more than a fifth of the country's entire cropland and supplies over 3/4 of the nation's feed grain and silage nutrients. The processing of corn in this country alone supplies over 3 million tons of human food a year.

The common corn plant goes right on building civilizations.

Then was the creation and the formation. Of earth, of mud, [our Forefathers] made man's flesh. But they saw it was not good. It melted away, it was soft, did not move, had no strength ... At first it spoke, but had no mind. Quickly it soaked in water and could not stand. And the Creator and the Maker said: "Let us try again because our creatures will not be able to walk or multiply...."

[Then] the figures were made of wood. They looked like men, talked like men, and populated the face of the earth .... but they did not have souls, nor minds, they did not remember their Creator, their Maker ... they had no blood, nor substance, nor moisture, nor flesh; their cheeks were dry ... Immediately the wooden figures were annihilated, destroyed, broken up, and killed....

And then grinding the yellow corn and the white corn, Xmucané made nine drinks, and from this food came the strength and the flesh, and with it they created the muscles and the strength of man ... the arms and legs of man. Only dough of corn meal went into the flesh of our fathers, the four men, who were created.

The creation of man, from the
*Popol Vuh: The Sacred Book of the
Quiché Maya.*

From the translation of Adrian Recinos.
Copyright 1950 by the University of
Oklahoma Press.

Santa María de Jesús. Grinding corn

Zacualpa

The grain with which they make their bread is a kind of pea, and there is white, crimson, black and reddish. Planted, it produces a high cane like a half pike, which gives two or three ears where the grain is...

Description of corn written by a
companion of Cortes in Mexico

[To prepare] this bread for eating, they cook the grain in water, mash, grind, and knead it; and they either cook it, wrapped in leaves in hot ashes (because they do not have ovens) or they roast it over live coals.

Francisco López de Gómara
Sixteenth century European herbalist

What does the feel of soil and sweat, of a pine-handled hoe and dried corn husks do to a man? How might he be affected by the oozing of soft mud and tender weeds between his toes, the slap of rough-edged corn leaves across his face, and the grittiness of dust and corn pollen in his hair? Is he not likely to feel a touch of pride as he watches the bagful of seed he has planted turn into a field of stout, ten-foot corn plants? Is there not a simplicity and directness in growing one's own food—a special satisfaction in being able to feed one's family with the fruit of one's own labors?

I suspect that a life spent among the cornfields would create in a man a sense of simplicity, satisfaction, and pride. And of closeness to nature and the earth.

Rabinal

2
INSIDE ADOBE WALLS:
The Home and Family

Sololá

The highland cities that were still inhabited when the *conquistadores* arrived had one striking feature in common: they were extraordinary natural fortresses. Iximché, Zaculeu, Utatlán, and Mixco Viejo were all surrounded on three sides by 300- to 500-foot cliffs nearly impossible to climb. Before the Conquest, high walls and heavy gates protected the more exposed approaches. Inside the gates, experienced, battle-hardened armies stood ready to defend their homelands. With the coming of the Spanish, however, the cliffs were scaled, the walls destroyed, and the defenders defeated. The Indian people were stripped of every means to defend themselves except their thick-walled adobe homes. And their secrecy.

During the four centuries since the Conquest, the Indian people have learned that secrecy is still their best defense. If they own anything of value, their surest protection against its being taken away is that it remain a secret. If they love someone, they best avoid being hurt by letting no one know whom they love, or how much. If they hate someone, they can most easily avoid reprisals and recriminations by hiding their feelings from the one they hate. And if no one ever finds out how much they know and understand, they will be passed off as ignorant and dumb—of no potential threat to anyone—and will more likely be left alone to live their lives in peace. Being dismissed as "taciturn," "ignorant," and foolishly "all-suffering" is, after all, a small price to pay for survival.

Nevertheless, once an Indian finds himself safe within his home—once the presence of just his family and trusted, well-proven friends makes his secrecy unnecessary, he can allow his true feelings to be exposed. Here, within the security of his own home, the man who all day long has seemed dull and unperceptive can laugh and play with his children for hours. Here, in his home, the same man who didn't seem to understand that he was being insulted and laughed at during the day will carry on for half an hour about the uncultured brutes who never learn to keep their mouths shut. And here the young husband who all day long acted as if he hardly knew his wife can show her the quiet tenderness he really feels.

The home is the vital center of Indian life—the place where, unafraid and uninhibited, the Indian people can be themselves with those they trust and those they love. Here is where the real interplay of Indian life takes place, the true quality of Indian life is revealed.

The home is also the place in which Indian culture, with all its customs, traditions, legends, hopes, and values, is preserved. Here, during endless hours of work and instruction, in a process as old as the Indian culture itself, the children learn the skills, attitudes, feelings, and identity that will shape their lives. The Mayan life will, thus, have passed to yet another generation.

THE CHILDREN

"These children can play for hours with the simplest toys and never look bored or unhappy."

A dozen visitors to Guatemala have made this comment to me about the children in rural Indian villages. Many of them have also mentioned the children's obedience to their parents, their willingness to help with family chores, their lack of need for attention, and their bright, excited cheerfulness. Indian children seem to show so many signs of happiness, security, and emotional health.

Part of the reason undoubtedly lies in the nature of task-simple cultures in general. The absence of a need to compete with others and the low amounts of criticism and failure they have to face would obviously contribute to a sense of emotional well-being. But Indian children also grow up within a network of close personal relationships. These relationships, with their community, their parents, and their brothers and sisters, give the children a feeling of acceptance and approval.

In traditional areas, villages as a whole generally maintain close ties. In more progressive areas, villages have often split over issues connected with potable water projects, road projects, or cooperatives. When this happens, groups of families within the community band together according to their common interests or blood relationships. In either case, the bonds that hold together groups of Indian families are strengthened by many forces that have long since been weakened or lost in many Western communities. First of all, groups of Indian families achieve a sense of solidarity through their common occupation. Nearly everyone earns his living from agriculture. The people thereby share common interests and worries, attitudes and problems. When the rains fail, everyone worries together; when the weather has been good and the corn is growing tall and green, everyone can share in the general rejoicing.

Poverty also pulls people together because it makes them feel that they are caught in a life and death struggle with nature. Life has taught them, sometimes cruelly, that no one can "go it alone." Everyone will need the help of his neighbors and community occasionally; maintaining good relationships with at least part of the community can be a matter of physical necessity. Discrimination produces similar results. The threat comes from another group of people rather than from nature or one's economic plight, but the normal human response to the threat is the same: to pull together in mutual defense.

Indian communities gain further solidarity because of the people's lack of mobility. Nearly everyone in an Indian village expects to stay in that village for the rest of his life, and expects nearly everyone else to stay there, too. Thus relationships have plenty of time to grow and mature. On the other hand, a man who creates enemies may have to live near them the rest of his life.

Indian children's sense of security is also reenforced by constant physical contact. For the first six to twelve months of a child's life, he spends most of his waking hours on his mother's back. During the rest of his childhood, he sleeps with his brothers and sisters and spends hours in the arms and laps of his mother, father, sisters, grandparents, and anyone else who lives in the home or nearby. As a youth, he will walk to work or school arm in arm with his companions just as naturally as he would shake hands with a new acquaintance. Such generous amounts of physical contact cannot help giving a child a sense of security and of being loved.

Emotional support for young children also comes from their brothers and sisters. A friend of mine used to say that if the study of psychology had originated among the Indian people, the term "sibling rivalry" would never have been invented. Children in traditional Indian families show few signs of jealousy or competition. This fact is partly due to the extended family system. Children feel less need to compete for attention because several adults are generally around the home; there are plenty of adults to go around. Furthermore, when the adults *are* at home, the children are their main source of entertainment. The grown-ups have no books or magazines to read, television to watch, or work to do from the office. They entertain themselves in the evenings by talking and playing with their children.

Brothers and sisters need not compete for toys, either. Homemade slingshots, pine needle necklaces, pop bottle caps, and clay marbles are seldom in such short supply that children need to fight over them.

Lastly, children in task-simple cultures find an important source of satisfaction in helping their parents with chores that are vital to the family's welfare. Children everywhere occasionally enjoy helping their parents with chores. But all too frequently in advanced economies they are able to handle only the low-status, menial jobs that contribute nothing to the family's income and just marginally to its basic welfare. Whereas ten-year-old children in the industrialized societies can neither help their fathers earn the family's living nor help their mothers do the more complex parts of child-raising and housekeeping, the children in task-simple cultures can help with almost any job.

Thus Indian children grow up in an environment with a maximum of physical contact, a minimum of criticism, competition, and failure, a lack of sibling rivalry, and a close feeling of belonging in their families and communities. In such an environment, how could they be anything but emotionally healthy?

Each evening when the fields have grown too dark to work and the footpaths too dim to follow, an Indian peasant family comes together at home. There the family crouches around the cooking fire on the dirt floor to eat dinner while weak, over-sized shadows waver against the smoke-blackened walls. Parents and children sip coffee from tin cups and use tortillas to scoop black beans from rounded gourds. They talk quietly, tease each other, and pass around the day's gossip. Eventually, as the children become sleepy, they quietly slip off one by one into the candle-lit corners of the room to lie down on matted wooden platforms where, snuggled between brothers and sisters, they go to sleep.

Such times remind me of childhood evenings spent sitting with friends around a campfire after a long day of hiking. The darkness is mystical, calm, quieting, even patient—a lot like the Indian people themselves.

Santa Catarina Palopó

San Juan Cotzal

34

It was midnight, February 4, 1976. As I neared the town of San Martín Jilotepeque, the moonlight reflected off a scene reminiscent of Dresden or Hiroshima after the war. The earthquake that had ravaged the highlands 21 hours earlier had turned the old colonial town into one long, uneven pile of broken roof-tiles, crushed adobes, and shattered wooden beams. Where 400-year-old cobble-stone streets had once passed, foot-worn trails wove over and around fallen adobes and splintered door frames. Groups of frightened survivors huddled around bonfires scattered amid the wreckage.

As I picked my way through the town, people called out, "You're alive! Are you all right?"

"Have you seen my son, daughter, nephew? Is he all right?"

"Where were you when it happened?"

Behind the questions lay a palpable sense of fear—fear that the injured would yet die, that other friends would be found dead, and that the awful shaking would never cease.

But I began to sense a subtler fear. Somehow a dreadful change had taken place—a vital part of the Indian people's lives had been turned upside-down. The homes that had once been their greatest source of security had turned into their most treacherous enemies. The same homes they had thought were their surest refuge had now become the killers of their families and friends.

Santo Domingo Xenacoj

Where passing years bring little change, today's children gr
up among the same fields, forests, and adobe walls, with the sar
customs, chores, diversions, needs, and fears as yesterday's ch
dren. Grandparents and their grandchildren walk the same v

trails, grow tired at the same work, worship the same gods, grieve over the same losses. Gaps have little chance to grow ween generations.

Santiago Atitlán

38

Touch comes natural to Indian youth. Years spent riding on their mothers' backs, crawling through the laps of relatives, and walking arm in arm with friends are not forgotten when different passions arise.

But a young girl's desire must be tempered by many cautions. Her parents have ideas about who should be her husband, and even stronger ideas as to who should not. (And they can make it hard for her to see those they think should not.) A young girl must make sure her lover's affection will be lasting, for she will need someone to provide for her once she has her children. And she is not just choosing a companion and a lover; she is deciding on a lifetime master.

So courtship becomes a time of testing, an endless series of evenings spent walking around the plaza or talking quietly in dark doorways. Her lover will kid and cajole, promise and flatter. And make frequent, flowery *declaraciones* of his undying love.

An anthropologist friend of mine had been studying an Indian village near Lake Atitlán for several months. One day I found him stumped by a problem that had come up in his statistics: the birth rate in the village had mysteriously dropped soon after 1965. He knew of no family planning programs, no major outbreaks of disease, nor any large emigrations. People just suddenly began having fewer children.

A couple of weeks later, he had figured out why. "That year the town finished its potable water project," he told me. "With spigots in every home, the teen-age girls no longer had any excuse to walk across town to the village well."

Patzum

San Martín Sacatepéquez (Chile Verde)

3
A DOLLAR A DAY

"How can these people be so poor?

At first you tell yourself that perhaps they are lazy, or are not very smart, or are just too set in their ways to *want* to achieve a higher standard of living. But then you suddenly remember how many thousands of acres of cornfields you have seen that were planted, weeded, hilled up, and harvested totally by hand. Or you get up at 6:00 A. M. and find Indian farmers already working in their fields. No, these people are not lazy.

In time, you meet several Indian people like Pedro Chacach. Never having had a chance to go to school, Pedro learned to read and write and earned a sixth-grade diploma by studying on his own evenings after work. In addition, he has taught himself to speak a fair amount of English and has become a first-rate farmer and one of the department of Chimaltenango's best "barefoot doctors". Lack of intelligence doesn't explain the Indian people's poverty very well, either.

Finally, you visit an agricultural development program that teaches local farmers techniques appropriate to their conditions and their resources, that teaches these techniques in ways the people can understand, and trains them to spread the word to their neighbors. The eagerness with which they learn, the enthusiasm with which they adopt new methods of production, and the phenomenal gains in production they achieve catch you by surprise. Traditionalism doesn't explain very much, either.

So the question remains: "Why are these people so poor?" The primary reason lies in the area's lack of thousands of factors which, in developed countries, work to increase the value of an individual's labor. The most obvious of these "work value increasers" (WVI's) are machines, such as trucks and tractors; natural resources, which include land, minerals, and fuel to make their machines run; and an economic infrastructure, which would include the roads over which the trucks and tractors must pass. Less obvious examples include improved methods of production, business organization, and management. Even less noticeable, but equally important, are social factors such as the absence of discrimination (so everyone is allowed to be productive), the equitable enforcement of the laws, and a pragmatic system of education. Without these WVI's, no man's work will earn much more than a dollar a day.

Alejandro Batz, an Indian farmer from a small village 15 miles from Sololá, grows corn and wheat on two acres of eroded hillside. His harvest each year comes to about $ 0.90 per day of work put into it. Were there a road to his village, he could sell his corn in town at a better price, making his work worth $ 1.10 a day. An educational system that would have taught him about chemical fertilizers could have helped him quadruple his harvests, raising his daily wage to over $ 3.00. Add a reasonable land tax and a government that could collect it fairly, and the owner of the 300 acres of flat land ½-mile away would either have to cultivate it for the first time, providing paid employment, or sell it to someone who would. Then Alejandro could earn $ 2.00 on those days he had no work on his own land. If Alejandro and his neighbors had access to credit, they could buy the land, a small tractor, and fertilizer—and raise their daily incomes to $ 10.00. Distribute a healthy industrial sector throughout the highlands, and the increased demand for food would raise the price of Alejandro's produce once again. His 90¢ day could be turned into a $ 15.00 day.

The United States was blessed 150 years ago with millions of acres of fertile land free for the taking. Those who settled these lands worked hard and often consumed sparingly; the WVI's they accumulated and left behind make our work more valuable today.

The wealth of the developed countries has been increased further by the WVI's they have imported from the less wealthy countries. In the past, conquest and colonization were responsible for immense transfers of wealth to the colonizing nations. Today, North American corporations control or decisively influence the use of over

70% of Latin America's raw materials resources. One-fourth of all our nation's corporate profits come from abroad. Every time a multinational subsidiary in Latin America sells goods to its foreign headquarters for less than the market value, every time corporations alter their accounts to show fewer profits and pay fewer taxes in Latin America, and every time the power, influence, or bribes of foreign concerns earn them a competitive advantage, the developing countries are drained of more WVI's. And, of course, the Indian people's WVI's can be drained away by other Guatemalans as fast as by foreigners—through economic, educational, and social discrimination.

The WVI's whose scarcity most impedes development in the more remote parts of the highlands are roads and educational opportunities. An illiterate farmer can neither collect nor remember the information necessary to substantially improve his agricultural production. Without roads, he has no incentive to produce a surplus because he has no way to sell it.

In more and more areas of Guatemala, roads and schools are common and are steadily being improved. The critical WVI for the Indian people in these areas is most often land. In an agricultural economy, land is not only the principal means of production; it is also the primary source of employment, social prestige, collateral for credit, and even political power. Huge tracts of uncultivated land are held from the market for purposes of speculation and investment. Other tracts are too large for Indian people to buy or are denied to Indian buyers whatever the price they offer. In these areas, many Indian farmers already have the technical know-how and resources to make the land produce well. Some Indian farmers with only ten acres already earn over $ 2,000 a year. They can afford decent homes, send their children to high school, and occasionally indulge in a television or motorcycle. But the vast majority of Indian people own fewer than half a dozen acres. Their children will not have enough land to live well in the village nor to educate themselves sufficiently to leave. Without land, they have little hope of ever escaping the poverty that surrounds them.

Many people feel that as long as a country has the right kind of government, the capitalist system will work. But, in fact, it may not. There are as many attitudes as there are laws that go into the proper functioning of capitalism. People must have a strong sense of individuality, a belief in private property, a basic sense of honesty, faith in a monetary system, and an ethic that puts a high value on hard work for individual gain. They must also have a value system that permits free trade and competition and sees the accumulation of unlimited material possessions as both positive and desirable.

These attitudes are not found in many traditional cultures. Among the Indian people in Guatemala, for instance, individualism is tempered by close relationships in the family and community. Nevertheless, the Indian people do possess most of these values, and are therefore referred to as penny capitalists.

San Pedro Sacatepéquez, San Marcos. Baking bread.

Each economy has an inertia of its own. Some have an inertia of motion. In these cultures everything is moving and shoving against everything else and forcing it to stay in motion. Steel mills roll out steel that is shipped to the auto industries, which mold the steel into cars that are rushed to dealers who must sell them to the millions of people who must buy them so that they, too, can remain in motion. In these cultures the adjectives "hard-working" and "industrious" are automatically taken as compliments, and speed and efficency are considered virtues, even after the purpose for all the motion has been forgotten.

But in Guatemala, the inertia is that of a body at rest. Here the life is *tranquilo,* as they proudly say in Spanish. Come down to work for six months, and you will soon be complaining that nothing seems to move as it should—that it is impossible to get anything moving on its own in only six months. But stay around for a couple of years. Pretty soon you may realize that you have time here to do a lot of things you have always wanted to do. There's time to read a good book, to chat with the neighbors, to climb a volcano, or to go take a swim in the river. There is more time to talk with people, and to listen to them. And there is a whole country full of people who have time to listen to you.

You may find you like it here. I think something about the pace of life agrees with the human organism. (I know a good many North Americans who lived a few years in Guatemala and suffered more culture shock when they went *back* to the States than when they first came down.)

San Antonio Nejapa. Washing clothes

Almolonga. Market

More than 30,000 people live in the *municipio* of San Martín Jilotepeque. When the earthquake of February 1976 destroyed all the roads leading into the *municipio,* the town was left isolated for two weeks. Many of the town's supplies had been buried under the people's crumbled homes, and the emergency food brought in during that time could not have fed more than a few hundred people.

Yet the only goods that most of San Martín's 30,000 people missed during these two weeks were salt, soap, rice, matches, and cooking oil; everything else they needed they could produce themselves.

San Pedro La Laguna. Weeding onions

A group of Indian women in San José Poaquil had asked me to teach them how to plant and take care of a vegetable garden. We chose a place, laid out the beds, and planted several varieties of vegetables. Two weeks later, I returned to check on the watering and weeding. The watering had evidently gone very well, because the weeds had grown so thick I couldn't find the vegetables.

The women crowded around me as I began showing them how to weed a garden. But just as I started to pull out the first weed, a dozen women gasped in unison, "Oh, no! Don't pull out that one! It's really good for curing headaches."

As I reached for a second weed, "Careful! That one is good for dyeing cloth." And, of course, the next weed was just delicious when stewed with tomatoes, and the following one was used for stopping the bleeding when a person had been injured. Finally, I let the women teach *me* which plants to pull and what each plant we left was good for.

Over the years, through a good many similar experiences, the Indian people taught me that in their own environment and among their own problems, they are often a lot wiser—and a lot more knowledgeable—than I am.

Soloma. Carding and spinning wool

San Antonio Aguas Calientes. Weaving a *huipil*

The Mayas of Yucatán are very generous and hospitable, since no one enters their houses without him being offered food and drink ... and if they do not have any, they go out to ask for some in the neighborhood. And if travelers join them on the roads they must give to all, though they may have much too little for this.

Diego De Landa
Sixteenth century Spanish bishop

San Antonio Palopó

Nahualá

4
MOUNTAINS MARKED WITH CROSSES:
Beliefs and Social Attitudes

A pediatrician working in the town of San Juan Sacatepéquez noticed that dozens of the infants he examined had damaged or bleeding palates. Mystified at first, he eventually discovered the reason. Many diseases of small children cause diarrhea and vomiting, both of which dehydrate the child. Dehydration, in turn, causes the soft spot in a child's head to sink inward (a condition called *mollera hundida).* Having observed that their ailing children often had *molleras hundidas,* the Indian people have mistakenly, though understandably, come to the conclusion that the *mollera hundida* caused the diseases, rather than the other way around. Therefore, they try to prevent their children from becoming ill by making sure that the soft spot does not sink inward. This can be achieved by pushing upward with one's thumb on the baby's palate.

Like that of the *mollera hundida,* many Indian beliefs which seem strange to us have simple, surprisingly logical explanations. Another belief very common throughout the highlands is that *gringos* (a word applied, with no negative connotations, to all light-skinned foreigners) are cannibalistic. We reputedly have a particular fondness for young children.

As far as I can tell, this belief traces its orgins to the gypsies that roamed the Guatemalan highlands up until about fifty years ago. These gypsies were noted for their abilities at raising, riding, and trading horses. They also had a reputation as master thieves—of food, horses, chickens, tools, and anything else one didn't keep an eye on—including children. Since scarcity of food is a common problem among Indian people, they assumed that the gypsies stole the children for the purpose of replenishing their larders. The light-complected foreigners who roam Guatemala today are no longer the gypsies of horse-trading fame, but they have apparently inherited their predecessors' reputation for including an occasional child in their diet.

Another widespread belief is that of the evil eye. Indian parents often hesitate to show their small children to perspiring or inebriated men, menstruating women, or *gringos*. These people are all believed to have the power to bring illness or sudden death to children. To prevent their children from being evil-eyed, parents tie red strings or bracelets around their children's wrists and keep red caps on their heads. The origin of the belief in the evil eye is no mystery at all. The belief was prevalent among our own ancestors in Europe during the Middle Ages and was transplanted to the Americas by the *conquistadores.*

The most difficult feature of the Indian cosmos for most Westerners to accept is its abundance of supernatural beings. Spirits of people, plants, animals, and even rocks leave their hosts to wander through forest and village. Ghosts of the dead haunt houses and stand guard over the fabulous treasures buried by the Maya when the Spaniards arrived. And the whole procession of Christian saints, along with lords of the streets, the churches, the mountains, and about everything else, protect or punish those who cross their paths. We Westerners chuckle a bit at such goings-on. After all, science has taught us that supernatural beings do not exist.

For science, however, the nonexistence of supernatural beings is only assumed. If such beings did exist, the conclusion of every scientific experiment would be placed in doubt. Benjamin Franklin could never have been sure whether it was the lightning or a playful gremlin that sent the bolt of electricity down his kite string. And Mendel would have had to admit that, apart from the possibility that laws of genetics had determined the colors of his pea blossoms, he might have been fooled by a mischievous hobbit with a can of spray paint. Reluctant to work with such uncertainty, science long ago adopted a principle known as "parsimony," by which all phenomena would be explained in the simplest manner consistent with all the observed facts. In a single stroke, gremlins, goblins, ghosts, and disembodied spirits were done away with.

For many people, parsimony has gradually become more than just an intellectual expedient; the "Let's see what would happen if we assumed..." has been converted into an outright "Supernatural beings do not exist."

Yet scientifically observed phenomena keep flying in the face of parsimony-as-fact. Electrodes hooked up to plants record electrical impulses that react in consistent patterns to similar human actions. Certain people's unlikely predictions about the future come true more often than chance would warrant. Believers in Unidentified Flying Objects (UFO's) compile a growing mountain of evidence that strange machines are flying through our skies. And people who attend spiritual healing meetings recover from diseases that our best medical experts had pronounced hopeless.

As a result, many of us have come to believe in parsimony-as-fact somewhat selectively. Some people believe that plants may have feelings but not spirits. Others admit that UFO's might exist, but reject the idea of unknown beings inhabiting our planet. And a good many of us believe in the greatest exception to parsimony of all—God. Yet a belief in God gives rise to further clashes with parsimony. Pope Paul VI tells us that true Christians must believe in the devil, and Billy Graham has written a book saying that angels not only exist but have wings and do errands for God.

When believing in angels, devils, and plants with feelings is respectable enough to sell books about them, why do we feel that believing in ghosts and corn plants with spirits is so outrageous? How do we know, for instance, that ghosts are not merely devils in disguise? There is a chance—just a chance—that the evidence in favor of parapsychological phenomena, UFO's, and even God may continue to accumulate to the point that scientists can no longer pass them off as curious aberrations in the laws of probability. It just could happen that science will gradually be pushed, kicking and screaming, into admitting that the only way left to plausibly explain these phenomena is to concede that unseen beings do exist. When we finally do arrive at that point, just as when Columbus "discovered" America, the Indian people will already be there to welcome us ashore.

"Hail, World, pardon my trespass. This is the day, this is the hour at which I have requested your light and fortune, and also the binders and bearers of weapons, men and youths, the marksmen, men and youths, and also the masters of pistols, the masters of knives, the masters of cutlasses, the slayers and butchers, the World president, the World minister, the World governor, the World judge, the World [mayor], the World Indian [mayor] ... the miraculous saints, the saints who send sickness and pain, and also those who go about in the cold tempest by day and by night. . . .

Santo Tomás Chichicastenango. Kissing a crucifix

Todos Santos Cuchumatán. Sacrificing a turkey

"Come hither! And also the thirteen, fourteen stars, the mountains r

osses, and also the female idols, the male idols...

"Come hither! And also God and our
patrons, Santo Tomás, San Sebastián, San José, Señor Sacramento,
María Rosario, María Dolor, San Miguel, the people of antiquity, Señor
Cristo, María Concepción ... the
lord of the streets and the plaza, the
lords of the church, of Calvario, of the
Campo Santo, of the prison and jail;
come hither. It is I, World. Perhaps
I shall be able to summon you, perhaps not. However many may be your
manifestations, all alike see us, hear
us! Be seated here and you will hear
what is the meaning of this, my [offering] which I have placed on this
table."

A summons to all the gods to
hear a prayer of sorcery to be
used against a thief. Prayed by
a farmer from Chichicastenango.
(Quoted from Ruth Bunzel's
Chichicastenango)

San Juan Atitán. Fiesta with a marimba

The superiority of males is unquestioned among the Indian people, and they give recognition to it in a thousand little ways every day. The husband is always given his choice of the family's food, and the largest share of it. When important guests arrive, the head of the household eats in the dining room or corridor with the visitors while the women and children eat around the cooking fire. During meetings, women often sit on the dirt floor while the men stand or sit on benches and chairs. And in many towns, women still walk several paces behind their husbands.

In the most traditional areas, even more customs acknowledge the superiority of males. Women take care to pile the family's dirty clothes so the males' clothes are on top. They avoid sweeping the floor in the presence of a man for fear the broom might accidentally pass over his foot. A woman in the marketplace will avoid stepping over a basket of corn so as not to damage the grain's masculinity. And a young fellow once passed up my offer of a free ride on a ferris wheel because the girls on it would be circling up over his head.

In many towns, however, these traditions are breaking down rapidly. Cristina, a young Indian girl from Chimaltenango, used to work in a little restaurant at which I often ate. Her quick sense of humor and good looks used to attract more than her share of the kidding from the male clients. One day as Cristina was cleaning up the dining room, a young Indian fellow was giving her a harder time than usual, and the rest of us were in fits of laughter. But Cristina was never at a loss for a comeback. "You'd better be careful," she laughed, "or I'll run this broom right over your foot."

Tecpán

69

Joyabaj. Indian mayor's office

Social disapproval in small, non-mobile communities is a stronger deterrent to unacceptable behavior than we might think. Among the Yucatán Maya of the sixteenth century, a man who had committed adultery with another man's wife could be punished in any way the offended man chose, including execution. The woman offender was considered sufficiently punished by having to go on living in a community where everyone knew what she had done.

Quezaltenango (Xelajú). Shoe store owner

5
ALL WINDS PASS AWAY

Then with the true God [of the Christians] ...
came the beginning of our misery. It was the beginning
of tribute, the beginning of church dues, the beginning of strife with purse-snatching, the beginning of
strife with blow-guns, the beginning of strife by
trampling on people, the beginning of robbery with
violence, the beginning of forced debts, the beginning
of debts enforced by false testimony ... This was the
origin of service to the Spaniards and priests, of service to the local chiefs, of service to the teachers, of
service to the public prosecutors by the boys, the
youths of the town, while the poor people were har-
assed.

The Book of Chilam Balam
of Chumayel

Throughout Mayan history, contact with outsiders has brought
nearly constant grief. The Indian people have learned to resist
foreign influences and, with the exception of the Roman Catholic
religion, have largely succeeded during the last 500 years.

Still, the outside world is pressing in on the Indian people as
never before. Roads penetrate farther and farther into the rural
areas; foreign development workers and missionaries can be
found in the most remote villages; and new schools are being built
every day. But the vanguard of this invasion is the transistor

radio. Perched on candle-lit shelves above cooking fires or hanging from tree limbs near groups of workers in the fields, the ever-present transistor radio sells cigarettes, chewing gum, and deodorants—and the values of a twentieth century consumer society. Little by little the people come to believe that beauty, popularity, and contentment are being sold at the village store. Without realizing it, they gradually become convinced that happiness can be bought and, even more damaging, that their own value as human beings is reflected in their ability to buy the accoutrements of a consumer society.

The lure of change has many allies. Feelings that their culture is inferior to Western culture, ingrained in the Indian people over hundreds of years, cause many of them to change to Western clothes and customs. The whip of not being able to compete with modern agriculture and industry spurs the people toward change almost as effectively as does the carrot of the comforts and luxuries they will be able to buy. And the desire, deep in the breast of every human being, to be considered well-informed and competent by those around him, pushes people to seek more knowledge and experiment with new patterns of living.

But for nearly five hundred years, a powerful array of forces has worked to preserve the uniqueness of Indian life. Prime among these forces is the belief in *destino,* a word that combines the meanings of the English words "fate" and "destiny." Most Indian people believe that a person's station in life is preordained—that a person is born into a role and must stay in that role. Poor people were made to do the work of poor people, while the rich were born to fill the stations of the rich. Centuries of teachings by the Catholic Church and others who benefited from the *status quo* have added to *destino* the belief that God creates people differently to serve different functions; no one should try to become something God did not intend him to be. Nor are some Protestants any more immune to using religion to keep other people down than are some Catholics. A well-to-do Protestant pastor near Chimaltenango repeatedly preaches that "economic improvement, especially through agricultural development, is the work of the devil."

Other forces also militate against change. Past experiences with foreigners have made any idea from the outside initially suspect. The people's first reaction to any such idea is usually, "What is *he* going to get out of it?" Gossip and peer disapproval, which have helped maintain the uniformity of Mayan culture for hundreds of years, can also be used effectively against those who wish to raise their incomes. Anyone who dares to be the first in his village to use chemical fertilizer or wear a neighboring town's *huipil* risks a barrage of criticism and social disapproval. The most frequently given reason for not doing anything differently is that "the people talk." And, of course, the many unsuccessful efforts to change which have been made in the past have instilled in many Indian people a deep sense of pessimism. One friend once told me, "When I first got married, I worked hard and built a really nice home. But a few years later it burned to the ground. I built a second home, but the owner of the large farm I lived on decided he liked it, and threw me out, without even letting me take my possessions with me. And now the earthquake has turned my third house into a pile of rubble." Under such conditions, fatalism is bound to flourish.

Lastly, among the very poorest, yet another force opposes change. Quite likely the most widespread and least understood psychological defense mechanism in the world is that of not facing the future. For millions of the world's people, every day is an eighteen-hour struggle to stay alive—to find enough food to eat, enough firewood to cook the food, and enough medicine to keep the malnourished children alive. These people can't afford to look ahead to the difficulties tomorrow might bring because today holds all the suffering they can bear. It is enough for them to deal with the problems of today—with the solutions of yesterday.

Clemente is a large, well-built man who can turn out as heavy a day's work as anyone. I have seen him top off a ten-hour work day by throwing four 125-pound sacks of wheat on a handcart, piling two more sacks on the back of his neck, and carrying all 750 pounds of grain the 1/4-mile to his house at nearly a trot.

Clemente's pride and determination are as strong as his 200-pound body. His father died when Clemente was in his early teens. With no land, he had to support his mother and five younger brothers and sisters. Through sheer hard work and determination, he not only provided for the whole family but earned enough extra money to buy twenty-five acres of land and a pickup truck.

One day, while walking through one of his wheat fields, Clemente began telling me about his mother. "She was always too poor to have decent clothes," he told me. "She was never able to go to school or even to eat well. When I was little, I used to watch how she suffered for my brothers and me. I always promised myself that someday she would have anything she wanted. Now I have bought her this land and have farmed it for her; I've kept my promise.

"But she is old now. Her body has suffered too many years of malnutrition and disease. I could give her all the things she ever longed for, but it's too late. She's too old and weak to enjoy it." As Clemente finished talking, tears stood in his eyes.

No one enjoys being poor. No one likes eating just tortillas twenty-one times a week, or having to go to bed without blankets enough to stay warm. I don't even believe anyone likes having to ask his own children to read a letter for him. There is pain in poverty. Most people who see a way out take it.

San Mateo Ixtatán. Walking to school

Cobán

After listing the injustices that the Spanish Conquest brought on the Indian people, *The Book of Chilam Balam of Chumayel* continues:

> But it shall come to pass that tears shall come to the eyes of our Lord God. The justice of our Lord God shall descend upon every part of the world, straight from God upon ... the avaricious hagglers of the world.

The longing that looked for God to work His justice still exists. Today it is more often given expression in the widely whispered rumor that Tecun Uman, the old Quiché king, continues to ride through the pine forests and adobe villages of the highlands, and that he may once again fight to free his people from their sorrow and distress.

The pain of a hundred thousand Clementes awaits retribution. Dreams of God's justice and of Tecun Uman's deliverance persist, fed by that pain—and by a deep-seated longing for the splendor, the wealth, and the dignity that once belonged to the Mayan people.

But change will not come easily to Indian society. The transition to a style of life like that of Gainesville, Guadalajara, or even Guatemala City could be difficult indeed for a people unaccustomed to criticism, competition, frustration, and failure—a people who depend heavily on close family and community relationships.

Imagine the future shock people would suffer if they tried to make in two decades the changes industrial societies have made over the past two centuries.

San Ildefonso Ixtahuacán

Who is to say, though, that Gainesville, Guadalajara, or Guatemala City has the kind of life Guatemala's Indian people need or want? Who can say that the European or North American style of twentieth century, or even that of Spanish-culture Guatemala, is the kind of twentieth century that would best suit the Indian people? In an era when countries from Tanzania to Laos and from Japan to Jamaica are clearly telling us that the Western way is not the only way, can we assume that our version of the modern life is the best for the Indian people of Guatemala?

The biggest problem ahead for the Indian people will not be that of deciding *whether* to change, but rather of deciding *what* and *how* to change. Which of the values and customs of Western culture should they adopt, and which should they reject? Which of the patterns of their own culture should they hold on to, and which had they best leave behind?

The future of Guatemala's Indian people, and of the nation as a whole, will be deeply affected by whether these questions are asked and how they are answered.

After the earthquake

Nahualá. Hoeing corn

"All moons, all years, all days, all winds, take their course and pass away."

An early Mayan prophet

During six years of agricultural development work, I have come to know many of the most progressive Indian farmers in Guatemala. Hundreds of them have learned to grow everything from bush beans, wheat, and potatoes to apples, cabbages, and tomatoes. Most of these men know very well that they can earn more money with any of these crops than they can with corn. Yet I do not know a single Indian farmer in the highlands who has land of his own and does not plant at least half an acre of corn.

Perhaps the rich, colorful patterns of Indian life must also take their course and pass away. But we can be sure that some of them won't do so for a long time to come.

Appendix

Each Mayan town in the highlands has its own traditional garb, or *traje.* This *traje* can be distinguished from the *traje* of any other town by its style, colors, patterns, or even its kind of weave.

Most of the *trajes'* designs are woven in as the material is made, although some are embroidered onto the cloth afterwards. Certain designs, especially on the *cortes,* or wrap-around skirts, are woven from tie-dyed thread known as *jaspe,* so as to form stripes of intermittent color or small figures.

Each town's colors, designs, and weaving techniques, passed from mother to daughter, invariably change over the years. In many towns, parts of the *traje* are no longer worn. In others, *trajes* as a whole (especially those of the men) have not been worn for so many years that no one remembers how to weave them; whole *trajes* have thus been "lost."

In addition to the *huipil,* or blouse, many *trajes* include a *sobre-huipil.* The *sobre-huipil* is worn over the regular *huipil,* either for warmth (see page 69), or during the performance of certain religious duties (as on page iv).

Front Cover. San Juan Sacatepéquez, Guatemala.* This *huipil,* the only one in Guatemala with dominant yellow and purple colors, is decorated with stylized birds. It is often worn with a belt and carrying cloth of the same colors. The dark *corte,* with light criss-crossed lines, can be seen beneath the apron. The *huipil* of *San Pedro Sacatepéquez,* near San Juan, is similar, but with dominant colors of purple and white.

Frontispiece. Aguacatan, Huehuetenango. A woman's hometown can often be determined by the hairpiece she wears or the way she wears it. Unique to Aguacatán is the broad, flat portion of the hairpiece that passes over the top of the woman's head. The

---

*The italicized names of towns at the beginning of each *traje's* description will be followed by the names of the *departamentos,* or states, in which the towns are located.

girl in this photograph, like Indian women throughout the highlands, is using the front of her *huipil* to carry personal belong-
ings.

Page vi. Nebaj, El Quiché. This picture shows Nebaj's ceremonial
sobre-huipiles in the lower left section and one of the two common styles of *huipil* in the upper right. The designs on the kind
of *huipil* not shown extend all the way around the garment.
The red *corte*, the multi-colored shawls and carrying cloths,
belts with geometric patterns, and twisted hairpieces (shown
halfway down the right edge of the picture) complete the *traje*.

Page x. San Juan Comalapa, Chimaltenango. This *huipil* can be
recognized by the two red stripes running along the shoulders.
Another, less traditional *huipil*, predominantly blue but with
similar figures, is commonly worn today. The *huipil* from
neighboring *San José Poaquil* has similar red stripes on the
shoulder, but can usually be distinguished from Comalapa's
because the Poaquil designs are greener and less elaborate.

Page 3. Sacapulas, El Quiché. Because of this town's warm climate, its white *huipil* is of lightweight cloth. It is identified by
the colored stripes that run horizontally across the back. When
in place, the hairpiece's large balls of yarn sit to one side of
the head. The *corte* is wrapped in such a way that no belt is
needed.

Page 6. Santa María Chiquimula, Totonicapán. A variation of
the *huipil* seen here has wide dark blue stripes separated by
narrow white stripes. As in many towns, some women from
Santa María Chiquimula wear white blouses with flowers embroidered around the neck. The dark blue *corte*, a little fuller
than most *cortes*, usually reaches clear to the ground.

Page 7. Zunil, Quezaltenango. Usually the *huipil* in this town is
purple rather than red, while the belt is normally red. The
corte, which often does not reach the knees, is the shortest in
the highlands.

Page 11. San Martín Jilotepeque, Chimaltenango. Also worn in
Chimaltenango, this *huipil* features an orange or yellow zig-
zagged "rainbow" that circles the *huipil* chest-high. As a variation, the entire *huipil* is sometimes made in purple and white.

Pages 14-15. Chajul, El Quiché. Adorned with small, stylized birds
or geometric figures, Chajul's *huipiles* may be red or white.
The *corte* is similar to Nebaj's. The men from Chajul, as well
as those from Nebaj and San Juan Cotzal, wear red wool coats
and red sashes. The designs on the coats and sashes differ from
town to town. The women of Chajul make their earrings by
passing foot-long strands of yarn through their pierced ears and

hanging silver coins on the yarn.

Page 21. Santa María de Jesús, Sacatepéquez. This *traje* is easily identified by the dark red and purple diamond-shaped pattern on the *huipil* and the distinctive *corte*. The older style of *huipil* has the same pattern, but with red diamonds on a white background.

Page 22. Zacualpa, El Quiché. The *huipil* from Zacualpa has purple shoulders over a red background. The *huipil* from Santo Domingo Xenacoj is sometimes confused with this *huipil,* but the shoulders of the Xenacoj *huipil* are generally brighter and more ornate. Stripes of various colors run horizontally across the top of the Zacualpa *corte* (seen behind the apron).

Pages 24-25. Rabinal, Baja Verapaz. The large cylindrical tufts worn in front of the head are unique to Rabinal. The traditional *corte,* not shown here, is similar to the red *corte* of Joyabaj and is worn without a belt. The Rabinal *huipil* ranges from an undecorated dark blue to a *huipil* similar to that shown on the young girl from Tecpán (see page 69).

Pages 26-27. Sololá, Sololá. The striped coat in this picture (which is worn only by religious elders), and the more common white coats, are adorned on the back with a stylized bat. The men's *rodillera* (the wool cloth that hangs from the waste to the knees), is similar to that of Nahualá, but is shorter. Sololá's *huipil,* like that of Santiago Chimaltenango (barely visible on page 6), has sleeves and is cut like a shirt, rather than like a *huipil.*

Page 33. Santa Catarina Palopó, Sololá. The shirt at the right is an older style, while the one at the left is more common today. The men's headdress is only rarely worn.

Page 34. San Juan Cotzal, El Quiché. This *huipil* is easily identified by its blue and green coloring. The belt is distinctive in that it is knotted rather than tucked in and has balls of yarn at each end.

Pages 36-37. Santo Domingo Xenacoj, Sacatepéquez. This photograph shows the difference between a fairly intricate Xenacoj *huipil* at the left, and a more common sample at the right. The child's red cap is typical of those worn in much of the highlands to protect them from being evil-eyed.

Pages 38-39. Santiago Atitlán, Sololá. The man's pin-striped shirt is handwoven. The traditional *corte,* which is red, is not shown, and, like those of Rabinal and Sacapulas, is worn without a belt. The woman's hairpiece consists of a strip of cloth about an inch thick and up to forty feet long. Only the last wind is embroidered.

Page 41. Patzum, Chimaltenango. The embroidered neck of this *huipil* can be either a geometric starburst or groups of flowers. The *sobre-huipil* from *Sumpango* bears resemblance to Patzum's *huipil,* except that the flowers in the Sumpango embroidery are smaller and more detailed.

Page 42. San Martín Sacatepéquez (Chile Verde), Quezaltenango. San Martín's *huipil* is made of material similar to the man's sleeve seen in the photograph. A San Martín man's outfit includes a brightly colored belt that hangs to the back of his knees, a dark wool *capixay* (like that on the man to the left on pages 64-65), and a long *tzute,* or headdress, which is seldom seen any more. The man in the photograph is carrying firewood and mustard greens.

Page 47. San Pedro Sacatepéquez, San Marcos. The most striking part of this *traje* is its unique yellow and green *corte.* The finest of these *cortes* are made of pure silk.

Page 49. San Antonio Nejapa, Chimaltenango. Now just a village, or *aldea,* Nejapa retains its *traje* from the time when it had the status of a town, or *pueblo.* The red and white striped background may include a third stripe of brown. The *huipil* of *Santiago Sacatepéquez* is similar to the red-and-white striped portion of this *huipil.* A group of cloth disks dangles from the front of the Santiago Sacatepéquez belt.

Page 50. Almolonga, Quezaltenango. Here we can see the similarity, yet variety, of patterns in the Almolonga *huipiles.* Another version of the *huipil* is predominantly yellow with small diamonds of red and blue, while simpler *huipiles* are only partly covered with the usual bright patterns, leaving visible the narrow vertical red and white stripes of the background material. In spite of the variation, the Almolonga *huipil* is generally recognizable for its dominant yellow, orange, and blue coloring and its simple, unbroken geometric pattern.

Page 52. San Pedro La Laguna, Sololá. We see in this shirt an example of the patterns made by tie-dying thread (called *jaspe*) before it is woven. Other examples of *jaspe* are seen in the photos on pages 24-25, 26-27, and 50.

Page 54. Soloma, Huehuetenango. The women of Soloma often add an Arabian touch to their *trajes* by fitting the head-hole of a second *huipil* over their heads and letting the whole *huipil* flow along behind them. The men's pull-over wool coat, known as a *capixay,* is used in many of the towns in the Huehuetenango area.

Page 55. San Antonio Aguas Calientes, Sacatepéquez. Wall hangings and other smaller weavings from this town are sold in Antigua and are very popular. The neighboring towns of *Parramos* and *San Andrés Itzapa* use a similar *huipil*.

Page 57. San Antonio Palopó, Sololá. The men's *rodillera* is similar to that of Nahualá (see page 84), but is longer. The trunk of the shirt usually consists of fine vertical red and white stripes with darker stripes every two to four inches. The sleeves are solid red with dark stripes. The *huipil* uses the same two patterns, but reverses them, the solid red section being in the center of the front and back portions of the *huipil*. The dark *corte* is worn quite long.

Page 58. Nahualá, Sololá. The majority of Nahualá's *huipiles* are simpler than the one shown. In fact, many are solid white with no decoration. The very fine geometric designs on the *huipil* are normally of a purple cast, the dyes of which often run onto the white background. The men's *traje* from Nahualá is shown on page 84.

Page 63. Santo Tomás Chichicastenango, El Quiché. The double-headed eagle, which traditionally adorned this *huipil* in the form of an abstract geometric design, is rapidly being replaced by flowers. The belt is also rapidly changing from a geometric design to a flower motif. The *corte* from Chichicastenango is made up of several sections of cloth held together by two bright-colored, two-inch-wide strips called *randas,* one of which passes behind the woman's hand in the photograph. Other towns, including Santa María de Jesús, Quezaltenango, Sololá, and Nahualá, have *cortes* with *randas* of different colors and widths. The carrying cloths of Chichicastenango (seen here holding a baby on woman's back and draped over the man's arm), vary in color and design. The men's wool *traje,* embroidered in silk, includes a fringed jacket, a bright tassled *tzute,* and short pants with colorful flaps on the sides.

Pages 64-65. Todos Santos Cuchumatán, Huehuetenango. A flat-brimmed hat similar to that of San Juan Atitán (see pages 66-67) is worn by both the men and the women of Todos Santos. The bandanas shown wrapped around the men's heads are seldom worn by younger men. The men's distinctive pants occasionally have additional stripes running horizontally, producing a plaid effect.

Pages 66-67. San Juan Atitán, Huehuetenango. The sides of the *capixay* worn in this town are open, as in a similar cape now only occasionally seen in *San Andrés Itzapa,* Chimaltenango.

Page 69. Tecpán Guatemala, Chimaltenango. Here, as in most of the towns in the *departamento* of Chimaltenango, the men's *traje* includes a square, fringed *rodillera*. The older woman is wearing a *sobre-huipil* from Tecpán, while the young girl is wearing the normal Tecpán *huipil*.

Page 70. Joyabaj, El Quiché. The men of Joyabaj may wear a long wool coat, like the man standing at the left, or they may wear an embroidered *rodillera*. The women may choose between the red *corte* shown in the photograph and a dark blue *corte* with stripes similar to those on the *corte* of nearby Zacualpa. The *huipil* may also vary, having either a deep blue or a striped red background.

Page 72. Quezaltenango (Xelajú), Quezaltenango. *Huipiles* from this town may come in combinations of purple, yellow, red, blue or green. These colors generally form horizontal lines, and many are finished with *randas* or with embroidered flowers running over the shoulders, as in the picture. *Cortes* are often dark-colored with narrow vertical stripes. Instead of being wrapped tightly around the hips, as in most towns, the *corte* from Xelajú is gathered at the top.

Page 77. San Mateo Ixtatán, Huehuetenango. The designs on this, one of the longest *huipiles* in the Guatemalan highlands, are embroidered rather than woven in. The large thickly-embroidered, red and yellow starburst design of the *huipil* is distinctive.

Page 78. Cobán, Alta Verapaz. This *huipil*, worn outside the *corte*, frequently has very fine embroidery around the collar and sleeves. The *corte* is worn gathered, as in Quezaltenango.

Page 81. San Ildefonso Ixtahuacán, Huehuetenango. The most obvious difference between this *huipil* and those of the nearby towns of *Colotenango* and *San Pedro Necta* is the distinctive pattern circling the neck of the Ixtahuacán *huipil*. The geometric design of the collar at the right is the traditional style, but many women prefer flowers, like those on the *huipil* to the left. A variation of *Ixtahuacán's huipil* contains narrow vertical red and white stripes throughout. The beautiful red *cortes* with horizontal stripes distinguish the *trajes* of several towns in the *departamento* of Huehuetenango from those of anywhere else in Guatemala. The *huipil* at the right is being worn inside-out, a custom widely used across the highlands to preserve the brilliance of the colors on the brighter side of the *huipil.*

The small figures shown at the beginning of each chapter are Mayan gods and goddesses of the pre-Conquest era. They are, in the order they appear:

Yam Kax, the maize god

Ix Chel, the goddess of weaving and childbirth

Ek Chuah, the merchant god

Itzamna, the head of the Mayan pantheon

Ix Ch'up, the moon goddess

BIBLIOGRAPHY

INTRODUCTION

Coe, Michael D., *The Maya* (Harmondsworth, Middlesex, England: Penguin Books, c. 1966).

Fuentes y Guzmán, Francisco Antonio de, *Recordación Florida,* quoted in Carmen Neutze de Rugg, *Diseños en Los Tejidos Indígenas de Guatemala* (Guatemala: Editorial Universitaria, c. 1974), p. 36.

Gallenkamp, Charles, *Maya, The Riddle and Rediscovery of a Lost Civilization* (New York, New York: David McKay Co., Inc., c. 1976).

Pagden, A. R., ed. and translator, *The Maya: Diego De Landa's Account of the Affairs of Yucatán* (Chicago, Illinois: J. Philip O'Hara, Inc., c. 1975).

CHAPTER 1: Corn, Soil, and Sweat

Finan, John J., *Maize in the Great Herbals* (Waltham, Massachusetts: Chronica Botanica Co., 1950).

Mangelsdorf, Paul C., *Corn: Its Origin, Evolution, and Improvement* (Cambridge, Massachusetts: Belknap Press of Harvard University Press, c. 1974).

Martin, John H. and Warren H. Leonard, *Principles of Field Crop Production,* 2nd edition (New York, New York: Macmillan Publishing Co., Inc., 1967).

Recinos, Adrian and Delia Goetz, translators, *The Annals of the Cakchiquels* and Dionisio Chonay and Delia Goetz, translators, *Title of the Lords of Totonicapán* (Norman, Oklahoma: University of Oklahoma Press, c. 1953).

————, *Popol Vuh: The Sacred Book of the Ancient Quiché* (Norman, Oklahoma: University of Oklahoma Press, 1950).

Wallace, Henry A., and William L. Brown, *Corn and its Early Fathers* (Ann Arbor, Michigan: Michigan State University Press, c. 1956).

CHAPTER 3:   A Dollar A Day

Lindqvist, Sven, *The Shadow: Latin America Faces the Seventies,* translated by Keith Bradfield (Harmondsworth, Middlesex, England: Penguin Books, c. 1972).

Myrdal, Gunnar, *The Challenge of World Poverty* (New York, New York: Pantheon Press, 1970).

Simon, Arthur, *Bread For The World* (New York, New York: Paulist Press, c. 1975).

Tax, Sol, *Penny Capitalism: A Guatemalan Indian Economy* (New York, New York: Octagon Books, 1971).

CHAPTER 4:   Mountains Marked With Crosses

Bunzel, Ruth Leah, *Chichicastenango: A Guatemalan Village* (Seattle, Washington: University of Washington Press, 1952), p. 370.

Hinshaw, Robert E., *Panajachel: A Guatemalan Town in Thirty-Year Perspective* (Pittsburgh, Pennsylvania: University of Pittsburgh Press, 1975).

CHAPTER 5:   All Winds Pass Away

Roys, Ralph L., *The Book of Chilam Balam of Chumayel,* new edition, (Norman, Oklahoma: Oklahoma University Press, c. 1967), p. 79.

Roland, 32, and Roger Bunch, 24, bring us nine years' experience of living and working with the Mayan people in highlands Guatemala.

Roland, with an M.S. in International Agricultural Development, has worked with the Indian people of the *departamentos* of Chimaltenango, Sacatepéquez, El Quiché, and Sololá. Roger, a freelance photographer, took these photographs during 1976. Both are natives of California.